WRITE!

Foundations and Models for Proficiency

M000248065

FOR THE STUDENT

WRITE! gives you the tools to be a better writer. You will enjoy writing more.

FOUNDATIONS

In Part I, you will learn about words. You will see how they are used in sentences. You will also study models of many kinds of writing. You will even do some writing of your own!

MODELS

In Part II, you will use what you have learned in Part I. You will study models of four different forms of writing. For each form of writing, you will

- see prompts and writing models.
- do your own writing, with tips for help.
- work with a partner to improve your writing.
- make connections between writing and other parts of your life.

So, let's start to *WRITE!*

Acknowledgments

Product Development

Maureen Sotoohi *Project Editor*

Dale Lyle *Project Editor*

Joan Krensky *Project Editor*

Jo Pitkin *Editor*

J. A. Senn *Content Reviewer*

Design and Production

Susan Hawk *Designer/Illustrator*

Yvonne Cronin *Typesetter*

Diane Dumas *Typesetter*

Illustration Credits

Illustrations by Susan Hawk

Pages 24, 53 Clipart.com

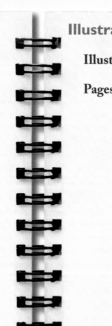

ISBN 978-0-7609-2458-7

©2004—Curriculum Associates, Inc.

North Billerica, MA 01862

TABLE OF CONTENTS

NOUNS

THINK ABOUT

You use words when you write. Some words name people, places, or things. These naming words are called **nouns.**

People		Places		Things	
girl		garden		apple	
teacher		town		balloon	

STUDY A MODEL

**Ms. Perez wrote a weather report.
Read the report.**

Your sister and brother need boots.

Rain falls in the city.

Snow falls in the country.

The words sister and brother name people.

The words city and country name places.

The words boots, rain, and snow name things.

PRACTICE

Match each noun with its picture.

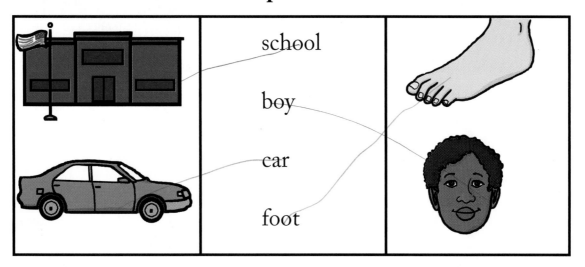

school

boy

car

foot

WRITE

Finish the weather report. Use nouns from the box.

mother   city   cloud   sun   rain

The _____sun_____ shines now.

A big _____cloud_____ will come.

Some _____rain_____ will fall.

Rain will fall in the _____city_____ .

Your _____mother_____ needs a hat!

PROPER NOUNS

Some words name special people, places, or things. These words are called **proper nouns**. Proper nouns begin with capital letters.

Special People	Special Places	Special Pets
 Dr. Hall	Park City	Max
Kevin	Silver Lane	Goldy

STUDY A MODEL

Kel made a map. Look at his map.

Smith School and Sand Street are special places. Each word begins with a capital letter.

Patty is a special person. Patches is a special dog. Each name begins with a capital letter.

PRACTICE

Match each proper noun with its picture.

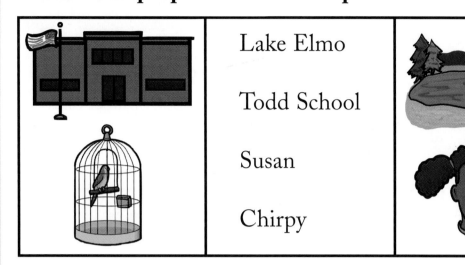

Lake Elmo

Todd School

Susan

Chirpy

WRITE

Finish the map. Use proper nouns from the box.

Golden Market	Spots	Cody	Green Street

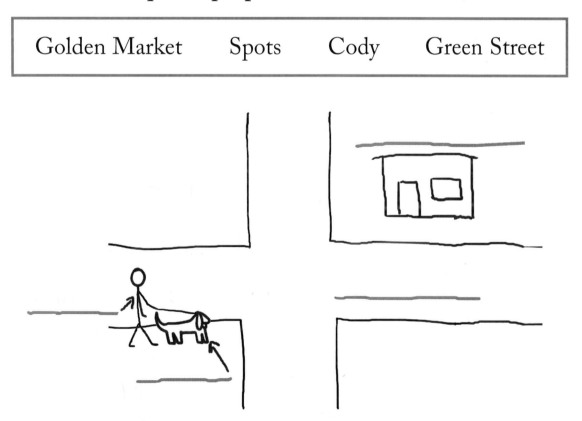

PLURAL NOUNS

THINK ABOUT

Nouns can name one or more than one. Nouns that name more than one person, place, or thing are called **plural nouns**. Add **s** to most nouns to make them name more than one.

One	clown	school	apple
More Than One	clown**s**	school**s**	apple**s**

STUDY A MODEL

Ana is on a picnic. She lists things she sees. Read her list.

3 ants

6 trees

2 melons

1 bird

2 lakes

Add **s** to ant to show more than one.

Add **s** to tree to show more than one.

Ana sees one bird. Do **not** add an **s** to bird.

Add **s** to lake to show more than one.

PRACTICE

Write the correct plural noun for each picture.
Use the plural noun from the box.

| girls | plates | bees | clouds |

1. _____

2. _____

3. _____

4. _____

WRITE

Help Ceci write her list. Use nouns from the box.
Add s to each noun to make it a plural noun.

| orange | bat | cookie | cup |

three blue _____

four juicy _____

two sweet _____

two wooden _____

PRONOUNS

THINK ABOUT

Some words take the place of nouns. These words are called **pronouns**.

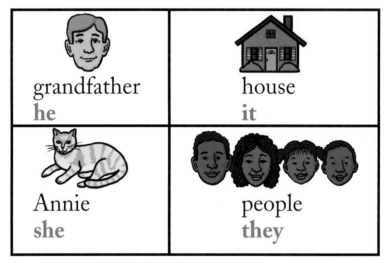

| grandfather he | house it |
| Annie she | people they |

STUDY A MODEL

**Marco wrote about a dog.
Read his report.**

Balto

Balto was a good dog. He helped

children. They were sick. They needed

medicine. It would save their lives.

He is a pronoun. It takes the place of **Balto**.

They is a pronoun. It takes the place of **children**.

It is a pronoun. It takes the place of **medicine**.

PRACTICE

Circle the pronouns that take the place of the words in red.

1. The truck goes down the road.

   It goes down the road.

2. Maria plays in the park.

   She plays in the park.

3. Where did the children go?

   Where did they go?

4. Joe likes to swim.

   He likes to swim.

WRITE

Finish the report about Balto. Use pronouns from the box.

He	They	It	They

The airplane could not fly. _____

was broken. Balto had to pull the medicine on his sled.

_____ ran very fast. Balto and the other

dogs ran in cold weather. _____ all ran

in deep snow. _____ saved the children!

USING I

THINK ABOUT

The word **I** is a pronoun. Use the word **I** to talk about yourself. Write the word **I** with a capital letter.

I eat ice cream.

I am sticky!

Always name yourself last.

Butch and **I** eat ice cream.

Butch and **I** are sticky!

STUDY A MODEL

**Shelly wrote a letter. Read her letter.
Look for the word I.**

Dear Grandma,

　　I went to the beach with Tom. Tom and **I** had fun! **I** made a sand castle. Tom and **I** ate hot dogs. We were tired!

　　　　　　Love,
　　　　　　Shelly

Shelly uses the pronoun **I** to tell about herself.

The pronoun **I** is a capital letter.

Shelly names Tom first and herself last.

12

PRACTICE

Check the ☐ after each correct sentence.

1. My friends and I went to the beach. ☐
   I and my friends went to the beach. ☐

2. I and Kara jumped in the water. ☐
   Kara and I jumped in the water. ☐

3. I and Jana played with a ball. ☐
   Jana and I played with a ball. ☐

4. Matt and I fed a bird. ☐
   I and Matt fed a bird. ☐

WRITE

Read the letter. Write the name and I to finish each sentence.

Dear Grandma,

    I read a book with Bo. _____ and _____

read a book. I made a picture with Alec. _____ and

_____ made a picture. I wrote a story with Kimi.

_____ and _____ wrote a story. I sang a song

with Chan. _____ and _____ sang a song.

                Love,

                Rob

VERBS

When you write, you use words that tell what someone or something does. These are action words. Action words are called **verbs**.

fly

eats

digs

STUDY A MODEL

The children are putting on a talent show.
Read the talent show program.

The children **tumble**.

Kiko **sings** and **plays** a drum.

The people **clap**.

The verb **tumble** tells what the children do.

The verbs **sings** and **plays** tell what Kiko does.

The verb **clap** tells what the people do.

PRACTICE

Match each verb with its picture.

paints

zips

quack

swim

WRITE

Write the verb that finishes each sentence.

plays	shout	dance	juggles	tells

Randy _____ jokes.

Dino _____ three balls.

Tina _____ the flute.

Two girls _____ on the stage.

The noisy fans _____ .

VERBS NOW

THINK ABOUT

Verbs tell what someone or something does. Verbs also tell you when an action happens. Some verbs tell what someone or something is doing **now**.

Luci **bakes** a cake now.

Today I **make** a pie.

STUDY A MODEL

Emilia is on vacation. She writes a postcard to Marie. Read the postcard.

Dear Marie,
    I **like** camping. I **sleep** in a tent. My father **builds** a fire. We **cook** outside.
        I **miss** you!
            Love,
            Emilia

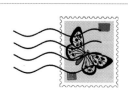

Marie Perry
496 Summer Road
Newton, NH 03062

Emilia is on vacation now.

Each verb shows what is happening now.

PRACTICE

The verb in each sentence shows what is happening now.
Circle the verb.

1. The rabbit runs fast.

2. The turtle walks down the street.

3. The rabbit sleeps under a tree.

4. The turtle wins the race.

WRITE

Write the verb that tells what is happening now.
Use the verbs in the box.

| mix | pulls | write | jumps | dances |

Today Nina _____ rope in the park.

Today we _____ our names on our papers.

Today Erik _____ to the music.

Today I _____ flour and water.

Today Dad _____ the wagon.

VERBS IN THE PAST

THINK ABOUT

Some **verbs** tell what is happening now. Other verbs tell what happened in the **past**. Add **ed** to most verbs to show what happened in the past.

Yesterday I **planted** some flowers.

Yesterday Ravi **watered** the flowers.

STUDY A MODEL

Last week the class had a clean-up day at school. Read about the clean-up day.

We **tossed** trash into big boxes.

We **cleaned** the playground.

We **fixed** the broken swing.

At the end we **played** baseball.

Clean-up day was last week. Last week is in the past.

All the verbs show what happened in the past.

All the verbs end with **ed**.

PRACTICE

Circle the verbs that tell what happened in the past.

1. Yoshi walked down the street.

2. He waited at the corner.

2. He crossed at the light.

4. Tory called to Yoshi.

5. The two friends talked.

WRITE

Write the correct verb to finish each sentence.
Use the verbs in the box.

| worked | planted | fixed | cleaned | painted |

The children _____ a broken window.

They _____ flowers in the garden.

The children _____ a fence white.

Two children _____ the messy playground.

They _____ for a long time.

SPECIAL VERBS

THINK ABOUT

You add **ed** to most **verbs** to show what happened in the **past**. Other verbs change in special ways to show what happened in the past.

Now

Now I **find** a pencil.

I **do** my homework now.

In the Past

Last night I **found** a pencil.

I **did** my homework after dinner.

STUDY A MODEL

Courtney had a birthday party. Read her letter.

Dear Athena,

I am sorry you missed my party. We saw a show. We played games. We went to the pizza place. Then we ate birthday cake.

Your friend,
Courtney

Miss and play are not special verbs. They end with **ed** to show what happened in the past.

See changes to saw to show what happened in the past.

Go changes to went.

Eat changes to ate.

PRACTICE

Check the ☐ after each sentence that tells what happened in the past.

1. Our dads make pizza. ☐
   Our dads made pizza. ☐

2. We ate it all. ☐
   We eat it all. ☐

3. I give a piece to Bert. ☐
   I gave a piece to Bert. ☐

4. I find empty plates. ☐
   I found empty plates. ☐

WRITE

Finish the letter about the birthday party. Choose the verbs that show what happened in the past.

We _____ a craft project.

do	did

Then we _____ on a hunt.

go	went

Our team _____ the treasure.

find	found

I _____ my friends treat bags.

gave	give

They _____ the bags home.

take	took

VERBS WITH ONE OR MORE THAN ONE

THINK ABOUT

Some **verbs** tell what **one** person or thing is doing. These verbs end in **s**. Some verbs tell what **more than one** person or thing is doing. These verbs do not end in **s**.

One

More Than One

One girl **skates**.

Three girls **skate**.

STUDY A MODEL

Lisa takes a trip to the zoo.
She lists what she sees.

One bear plays.

Two bears roll a ball.

One turtle swims.

Three tigers jump.

One lion roars.

The verbs plays, swims, and roars each tell what one animal is doing. An s ends each verb.

The verbs roll and jump each tell what more than one animal is doing. They do not end in s.

PRACTICE

Circle the correct verb to finish each sentence.

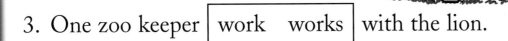

1. One girl | pet   pets | the lamb.

2. Two boys | pet   pets | the cow.

3. One zoo keeper | work   works | with the lion.

4. Two zoo keepers | work   works | with the bears.

WRITE

Finish the list from the zoo trip.
Choose the correct verb from each box.

One zebra _____ in the yard. | run   runs |

Two birds _____ at the food. | pecks   peck |

One snake _____ in his cage. | slide   slides |

Three monkeys _____ in the tree. | jumps   jump |

Four baby foxes _____ in a log. | sleep   sleeps |

23

USING IS AND ARE

THINK ABOUT

Is and **are** are **special verbs**. They tell about things that happen now. Use **is** to tell about one person, place, or thing. Use **are** to tell about more than one person, place, or thing.

Jack **is** a baker.

Dena and Miki **are** bakers too.

STUDY A MODEL

The T-ball team has a snack shop.
Read the ad for the snack shop.

The Tasty Treat Shop **is** now open. Our cookies **are** great. We sell drinks too. Milk **is** perfect with our warm cookies. We **are** ready for you. Come to our shop today!

The **Tasty Treat Shop** is one place. Use **is** to tell about one place.

Cookies are more than one thing. Use **are** to tell about more than one thing.

24

PRACTICE

Circle is or are to finish each sentence.

1. The brownies [is   are] on the tray.

2. This drink [is   are] cold!

3. The popcorn [is   are] fresh.

4. The three bags [is   are] full.

5. The girls [is   are] excited.

WRITE

Rasul wrote another ad for the snack shop. Finish the ad. Use is or are to complete each sentence.

The Tasty Treat Shop _____ open at eight.

Our cookies _____ so tasty. They sell out before nine!

Our bread _____ fresh. The workers _____

friendly. Our prices cannot be beat!

USING WAS AND WERE

THINK ABOUT

Was and **were** are **special verbs**. They tell about things that happened in the past. Use **was** to tell about one person, place, or thing. Use **were** to tell about more than one person, place, or thing.

One	**More Than One**
Her cap **was** new.	Her shoes **were** dirty.

STUDY A MODEL

Addie wrote a report about Jackie Robinson. Read her report.

Jackie Robinson **was** a baseball player. He **was** the first African American on a pro team.

Some people **were** angry when Robinson joined the team. No other players **were** African Americans. The team owner and the coach **were** kind. They wanted to give Jackie Robinson a chance.

Jackie Robinson was one person. Use **was** to tell about one person.

The **owner** and **coach** are two different people. Use **were** to tell about more than one person.

26

PRACTICE

Circle was or were to finish each sentence.

1. Last summer Lila and Ty | was   were | on a baseball team.

2. The team name | was   were | the Rockies.

3. The team shirts | was   were | blue.

4. Lila | was   were | the pitcher.

5. She and Ty | was   were | the best hitters.

WRITE

Addie wrote more about Jackie Robinson. Finish her report. Use was or were to complete each sentence.

Jackie Robinson _____ ready for his first game.

Many people _____ surprised to see him on the

field. But Robinson _____ a good player. Fans saw

how hard he worked. They _____ happy when he

did well. They started to cheer for him! Jackie Robinson

_____ a great baseball player.

27

ADJECTIVES

THINK ABOUT

Adjectives are words that describe people, places, and things. Adjectives can tell about **size, shape,** and **color.**

huge hippo

round cookie

pink coat

STUDY A MODEL

Dakota wrote a poem.
Read her poem.

I wonder what it is like
  up there so high.
The **tiny white** stars shine
  in the **dark** sky!
Could the **big round** moon
  be my home one day?
Would it be fun
  to live so far away?

The adjective **tiny** tells about the size of the stars.

The adjectives **white** and **dark** tell about color.

Big tells about size.

Round tells about shape.

PRACTICE

Write each adjective under the picture it tells about.

| round | square | red | small |

_____

_____

_____

_____

WRITE

Kari wrote a poem. Choose an adjective from the box to write on each line.

| green | round | huge | red |

Time to Go!

The _____ light means "go."

The _____ light means "stop."

These _____ lights keep me safe!

The _____ bus goes down the road.

Riding the bus is something I like!

MORE ADJECTIVES

THINK ABOUT

Some **adjectives** tell how someone or something **looks**, **feels**, and **sounds**.

Looks		bright sun
Feels		cold drink
Sounds		loud drum

STUDY A MODEL

**Angel wrote about his visit to the skating rink.
Read what he wrote.**

Skaters glide around the rink. They

wear **colorful** clothes. Their skates

make a **swishing** sound. One skater

falls on the **hard** ice. He gets up and

skates again.

The adjective **colorful** tells how the clothes look.

Swishing tells how the skates sound.

Hard tells how the ice feels.

PRACTICE

Write each adjective under the picture it tells about.

| quiet | wet | loud | sleepy | furry | sad |

_____   _____

_____   _____

_____   _____

WRITE

Look at the pictures above. Write two sentences about each picture. Use an adjective in each sentence.

_____

_____

_____

_____

31

OTHER ADJECTIVES

You have learned about **adjectives** that tell how someone or something looks, feels, and sounds. Other adjectives tell how someone or something **tastes** and **smells**.

Tastes	Smells
 sour lemons	stinky skunk
salty pretzel	fresh bread

STUDY A MODEL

Raul wrote about his sister.
Read what he wrote.

Last night my sister made soup. The **salty** soup tasted bad. So she added lots of pepper. The **spicy** soup tasted bad. Then she added sugar. The **sweet** soup tasted bad. My sister tried to make toast. The toast burned. Soon the whole house smelled **smoky**! Finally, we went out for dinner.

The adjectives **salty**, **spicy**, and **sweet** tell how the soup tasted.

The adjective **smoky** tells how the house smelled.

PRACTICE

Circle the adjective in each sentence that tells how something tastes or smells.

1. I took a bite of a sour apple.

2. I ate some of the spicy dip.

3. Who put their stinky shoes here?

4. Open the window and let in the fresh air.

5. Have a slice of this sweet watermelon.

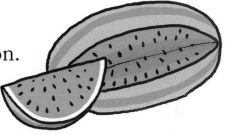

WRITE

Write about your favorite food. Tell how it smells and tastes.

My favorite food is _____. It smells

_____. It tastes _____.

I could eat my favorite food every day.

ADJECTIVES THAT TELL HOW MANY

THINK ABOUT

Adjectives can tell readers a lot about people, places, and things. Adjectives can tell **how many**.

one child   **three** kittens   **several** pencils

STUDY A MODEL

Read the math problem.
Then write the answer.

Tom had **three** pencils.

Lily had **two** pencils.

How **many** pencils did
Tom and Lily have?

Answer:

Three is an adjective.
It tells how many.

Two is an adjective.
It tells how many.

Many is an adjective.
It tells how many.

PRACTICE

Look at the picture. Then finish each sentence. Choose the correct adjective from the box.

| one | Four | Three | six |

1. This house has _____ windows.

2. It has _____ door.

3. _____ trees grow in the front yard.

4. _____ steps lead to the front door.

WRITE

Write about your house. Finish each sentence with an adjective that tells how many.

My house has _____ windows. It has

_____ doors. It has _____

rooms. _____ people live in my house.

ADVERBS

Adverbs are words that tell **how** something happens. Many adverbs end with **ly**.

Cross the street **safely**.

The crowd cheers **wildly**.

STUDY A MODEL

Chan wrote a recipe.
Read the recipe.

Crack the eggs gently.

Slowly stir the batter.

Spread the batter evenly.

Carefully put the tray in the oven.

Gently tells how to crack the eggs.

Slowly tells how to stir the batter.

Evenly tells how to spread the batter.

Carefully tells how to put the tray in the oven.

PRACTICE

Circle the adverbs in each sentence.

1. I can quickly clean the kitchen.

2. Pedro gently washes the glasses.

3. We happily swept the floor.

4. The dishes crashed loudly.

5. We looked at the mess sadly.

WRITE

Salim is making a sandwich. Finish each sentence.
Choose the correct adverb from the box.

Use the knife _____ . | careful   carefully |

Spread peanut butter _____ . | smoothly   smooth |

Put jelly on _____ . | lightly   light |

Cut the bread _____ . | slow   slowly |

Eat your sandwich _____ ! | happy   happily |

MORE ADVERBS

THINK ABOUT

Some **adverbs** tell how something happens. Other adverbs tell **when** or **where** something happens.

When

We go to the park **now**.

Where

We play **here**.

STUDY A MODEL

**Hector wrote about a party.
Read what he wrote.**

My birthday was yesterday.

My family had a party outside.

My father played the guitar. We danced

and sang songs. Later we had cake

and ice cream. It was a great day!

When was the party?
It was yesterday.

Where was the party?
It was outside.

What word tells you when everyone had cake and ice cream?

PRACTICE

Read each sentence. Circle the adverb that tells when or where.

1. The bus arrived early.

2. I came to school late.

3. Put the book back.

4. Lisa left her hat outside.

5. Today I will buy my lunch.

WRITE

Angie wrote about a race. Finish each sentence with the correct adverb from the box.

outside	here	Today	Soon

_____ I ran in a race. The race was _____

at my school. We ran _____ near the

playground. I ran fast. _____ the race was over.

I did not win the race, but I had fun!

CONTRACTIONS

THINK ABOUT

You can form a **contraction** by joining two short words. A **verb** and the word **not** can be joined to make a contraction. Use an **apostrophe (')** to take the place of the letter **o** in **not**.

are not = aren't | are | not | | aren't |

did not = didn't | did | not | | didn't |

do not = don't | do | not | | don't |

is not = isn't | is | not | | isn't |

STUDY A MODEL

Ms. Lenert's class made signs for the classroom. Read the signs.

These **aren't** for students!

We **didn't** forget to feed him.

Don't forget your homework!

This **isn't** a place to put books.

Aren't is a contraction. It joins **are** and **not**.

Didn't, don't, and isn't are also contractions.

The apostrophe (') takes the place of the **o** in **not**.

PRACTICE

Match the words to the contraction. Put in the missing (').

	Two Words	Contractions
1.	are not	don t
2.	do not	didn t
3.	did not	aren t
4.	is not	isn t

WRITE

Mr. Hayden's class made signs for the lunchroom. Write the contraction for the words in red.

Do not forget to clean up. _____

We did not forget to wash the table. _____

These tables are not for second graders. _____

There is not any dessert today! _____

Do not forget to eat fruit. _____

HOMOPHONES

Some words sound the same but mean different things. They also have different spellings. These words are called **homophones**.

The wind **blew** over the **sea**.

See the **blue** ocean.

STUDY A MODEL

Lian wrote a story.
Read her story.

No person won more cases than Sherlock Holmes. He would always know the answer to a problem. He would look for clues and write notes too. The mystery would be over in two or four days. How could one man always be right?

No sounds the same as know but is not spelled the same. These words mean different things.

Other homophones are won and one, for and four, and write and right.

To, too, and two are also homophones.

PRACTICE

Read the sentences. Circle the correct homophone.

1. Do you | sea   see | any fish?

2. The fish are in the | sea   see | .

3. I am going | to   two | the snack stand.

4. Can you get me | to   two | hot dogs?

5. The sky is very | blew   blue | .

WRITE

Jess wrote a story. Finish her story. Choose the correct homophone from the box.

My team went _____ the game. | to   two |

I got _____ goals. | for   four |

Did you _____ me? | sea   see |

We _____ the game. | won   one |

The crowd was happy _____ us. | for   four |

SENTENCES

THINK ABOUT

When you write, you put together groups of words. A **sentence** is a group of words that tells a complete idea. Every sentence begins with a **capital letter**.

Lou rides a bike.
He is going to the park.

Most sentences end with a **period (.).**

Always wear a helmet.
Helmets keep you safe.

STUDY A MODEL

Marshal wrote about a party.
Read what Marshal wrote.

We love class parties.

We play games.

One game is a relay.

We eat cookies.

We make crafts.

Each sentence begins with a capital letter.

Each sentence ends with a period.

PRACTICE

Write the first word of each sentence correctly.

1. the friends play baseball. _____

2. many players wear hats. _____

3. one boy throws the ball. _____

4. his sister misses the ball. _____

5. the sun is in her eyes. _____

WRITE

Write these sentences correctly.
Add capital letters and periods.

the students ride on the bus

_____

they go to the zoo

_____

the bears look sleepy

_____

the monkeys are funny

_____

PARTS OF SENTENCES

THINK ABOUT

Every sentence has two parts. The **naming part** tells who or what the sentence is about. The **action part** tells what someone or something does.

Naming Part	Action Part
Asad	puts on his socks.
The socks	fall down.
He	pulls them up.

STUDY A MODEL

**Cristina wrote about a class trip.
Read what she wrote.**

Our class went to an art museum.

The museum had many paintings. My

favorite painting showed a family. The

family lived long ago. Everyone wore fancy

clothes. The baby wore a long dress.

What is the first sentence about? The first sentence is about Our class.

What did the class do? The class went to an art museum.

PRACTICE

Match the parts of these sentences.

Naming Parts
The ship
Stars
The sailors on the ship
A tree

Action Parts
see an island.
grows on the island.
sails on the sea.
twinkle in the sky.

WRITE

You matched the naming parts and action parts of the sentences above. Now write the complete sentences.

_____

_____

_____

_____

_____

KINDS OF SENTENCES

THINK ABOUT

When you write, you use different kinds of sentences. **Statements** tell something. **Questions** ask something.

Happy Birthday!

Statements	**Questions**
The balloons are ready.	Does Ms. Wilson know?
We sent invitations.	Will she be surprised?

STUDY A MODEL

Paul wanted to know about the old days.
He asked his grandpa questions.

What did you do for fun?
We played games.

What games did you play?
My friends and I liked marbles.

What job did you do?
I milked the cows.

Questions ask something. A question ends with a question mark (?).

Statements tell something. A statement ends with a period (.).

PRACTICE

Write S if the sentence tells something.
Write Q if the sentence asks something.

 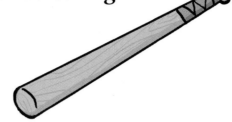

1. It is time for the game. _____

2. Are we going to warm up? _____

3. Is Juan playing first base? _____

4. Matt will pitch. _____

WRITE

Write three questions you might ask a friend. Write an answer for each question. Your answers should be statements.

_____ ?

_____ .

_____ ?

_____ .

_____ ?

_____ .

WRITING QUESTIONS

THINK ABOUT

How do you write **questions**? Changing the order of the words can sometimes turn a statement into a question.

Statements	Questions
The crayons were blue.	Were the crayons blue?
I may use a crayon.	May I use a crayon?

STUDY A MODEL

Inez wrote her grandmother a letter. Read the letter.

Dear Gran,

   I cannot wait to visit you. Will Aunt Rita be there? Will we go to the beach? I love to play in the sand. Do you have a bucket and a shovel? I will bring mine.

                    Love,
                    Inez

Inez changed these statements into questions in her letter.

Aunt Rita will be there.

We will go to the beach.

You do have a bucket and a shovel.

PRACTICE

Match each statement with a question.

Statements	Questions
Boats do go down the river.	Can tugboats pull large boats?
That boat is a tugboat.	Will we go for a boat ride?
Tugboats can pull large boats.	Is that boat a tugboat?
We will go for a boat ride.	Do boats go down the river?

WRITE

Change the statements into questions.

This is your favorite game.

_____ ?

You can teach me how to play.

_____ ?

We should play in the kitchen.

_____ ?

You do know how to play.

_____ ?

USING QUESTION WORDS

THINK ABOUT

You can also write a question by using a question word. The words **who, what, where, when,** and **why** are question words. Always put the question word at the beginning of the question.

Who found you?
What did you eat?
Where did you live?
When did you live?
Why did you go away?

STUDY A MODEL

**Zoe wants to learn about rain forests.
She wrote down questions.**

What is a rain forest?

Where are rain forests?

Who lives in a rain forest?

Why are rain forests important?

Use what to find out about a thing.

Use where to find out about a place.

Use who to find out about a person.

Use why to find out a reason.

PRACTICE

Circle the question word in each sentence.

1. Who sailed a ship?

2. What did the sailor find?

3. Where did he land?

4. When was his trip?

5. Why did he make this trip?

CHRISTOPHER·COLVMBVS

WRITE

What do you want to learn about? Write questions you want to have answered. Use each question word in the box.

| Where | What | Who | Why | When |

_____

_____

_____

_____

_____

CAPITALIZING THE NAMES AND TITLES OF PEOPLE

THINK ABOUT

The **names of people** begin with **capital letters**.

Katie Bridges   Terrel Jackson   Tram An

The **titles** of people begin with **capital letters** too.

Mr. Newman   **Dr.** Bell   **Mrs.** Santos

STUDY A MODEL

**Tina wrote about some people at her school.
Read what she wrote.**

Dr. June Weber is the principal of my

school. My teacher's name is Mr. Cole.

The music teacher is Miss Morris.

Ms. Ortiz is the gym teacher. Kara Lee

sits next to me.

Dr. and Mr. each begin with a capital letter. They each end with a period.

Miss begins with a capital letter. It does not end with a period.

First names and last names both begin with capital letters.

PRACTICE

Circle the letters that should be capital letters.
Then write the names and titles correctly.

1. My teacher is mrs. denton.

   _____

2. My doctor is dr. jones.

   _____

3. My neighbor is miss singh.

   _____

4. mr. amaro lives next door.

   _____

WRITE

Finish the sentences with the names of people you know.
Put capital letters and periods where they are needed.

My teacher is _____.

My gym teacher is _____.

_____ sits next to me.

_____ is my doctor.

CAPITALIZING THE NAMES OF SPECIAL PLACES

THINK ABOUT

Names of **special places** begin with **capital letters**.

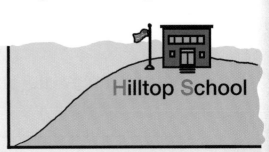

Fern Park

Silver Lake

Hilltop School

Main Street

Oak Street

Welcome to Bay City

STUDY A MODEL

Felix wrote directions to his home.
Read the directions.

Turn right on Sixth Street.

Pass Green Meadow School.

Go around Turtle Pond.

Go through Carl Park.

Turn left on Vine Road.

The names of all the special places begin with capital letters.

Look at the name Green Meadow School. Each word in the name begins with a capital letter.

PRACTICE

Check the ☐ after each correct sentence.

1. I live in coal city. ☐

   I live in Coal City. ☐

2. We go to Lincoln Elementary School. ☐

   We go to lincoln elementary school. ☐

3. Is goose lake near your school? ☐

   Is Goose Lake near your school? ☐

4. My school is on Grand Road. ☐

   My school is on grand road. ☐

WRITE

Cheryl wrote directions to her school.
Write the names of the special places correctly.

Start at willow lake. _____

Go around bluebell hill. _____

Walk on baker street. _____

Pass herman park. _____

Here is kennedy school. _____

CAPITALIZING THE NAMES OF DAYS AND MONTHS

Use **capital letters** when you write the **names of days**.

Sunday	Monday	Tuesday	Wednesday	Thursday	Friday	Saturday

Use **capital letters** when you write the **names of months**.

January 9

April 20

July 15

STUDY A MODEL

**Carly wrote about her trip.
Read what she wrote.**

In June my family went camping.

We put up our tent on Monday.

On Wednesday we swam. It rained

on Thursday. We came home on Friday.

In August we will go camping again!

June and August are the names of months. They begin with capital letters.

Monday, Wednesday, Thursday, and Friday are the names of days. They begin with capital letters.

PRACTICE

Circle each month or day that is written correctly.

1. Tuesday

   tuesday

2. march

   March

3. Friday

   friday

4. December

   december

5. sunday

   Sunday

6. September

   september

WRITE

Reese wrote about his trip. Write the names of the months or days correctly.

In february we went to a dog sled camp. _____

On monday we met the dogs. _____

We used snow shoes on tuesday. _____

We came home on saturday. _____

We will go again next january. _____

CAPITALIZING THE TITLES OF BOOKS

THINK ABOUT

The titles of books begin with **capital letters**. Use capital letters for the first word, the last word, and each important word in books titles. Also underline the titles of books.

Where Is My Dog?

A Baby Sister for Ali

Cowboy Tales

STUDY A MODEL

Sara keeps a reading log.
Read her log.

Reading Log

Title: Never Take a Pig to Lunch

Author: Nadine Westcott

This is a book of poems. All the poems are about food. They are all funny. I liked this book a lot.

Never Take a Pig to Lunch is the title of a book. Each important word in the title begins with a capital letter.

Little words like **a** and **to** do not begin with capital letters.

PRACTICE

**Find the book title in each sentence. Underline the title.
Circle the letters that should be capital letters.**

1. Last summer I read the lost bear.

2. Mr. Burns read windy willows aloud to the class.

3. tales of the sea tells about ships and sailors.

4. What do you think farm animals is about?

WRITE

**A reading log is where you write about books that you
have read. Finish this reading log. Write about two books
that you have read.**

Title: _____

Author: _____

What I liked: _____

_____

Title: _____

Author: _____

What I liked: _____

_____

CHECKING YOUR WRITING

Check your writing to make sure it is right. Find and fix any mistakes. Use this list to check for mistakes.

Checklist
Did I use **is** and **are** and **was** and **were** correctly?
Did I use capital letters correctly?
Did I put a period or a question mark after each sentence?
Did I spell the words correctly?

STUDY A MODEL

Bijan wrote a story.
Then he checked for mistakes.

my brother is in the band at hall high school. he plays the tuba do you know what a tuba looks like it is brass. it is bigger than i am

My brother is in the band at Hall High School. He plays the tuba. Do you know what a tuba looks like? It is brass. It is bigger than I am.

Begin each sentence with a capital letter.

Proper nouns begin with capital letters.

Put a period or question mark at the end of each sentence.

PRACTICE

Read the story. Circle the five words that should begin with capital letters. Put a period or a question mark at the end of each sentence.

Tomorrow i will see dr. soto I am not sick I am happy why am I happy to see this doctor Dr. soto is my grandmother

WRITE

Read the story. Circle seven mistakes. Then write the story correctly.

i like fishing with my dad We go out in our new boat We take drinks and many snacks just one thing is usually missing There are no fish

_____

_____

_____

_____

_____

PREPARE FOR A TEST

SELECTION 1

Read the story about a girl and her pet bird.
Then answer questions 1–10.

(1) nilda had a pet parrot. (2) The parrot's name was lucky.

(3) Lucky was coughing. (4) Nilda thought Lucky were sick. (5) So she and her mother taked Lucky to Dr. Torres. (6) Dr. torres was a special doctor for animals.

(7) Dr. Torres looks at Lucky. (8) Then he looked at Nilda.

(9) "How do you feel."

(10) "I dont feel sick now," said Nilda. (11) "Last week I had a bad cold."

(12) "Did you sneeze?" Dr. Torres asked Nilda.

(13) "Lots!" Nilda said.

(14) "Did you cough?" Dr. Torres asked.

(15) "Lots!" Nilda said.

(16) Dr. Torres smiled. (17) Nilda smiled to.

(18) "Lucky is making the same sounds I made!" Nilda said. (19) "Lucky isn't sick," she cried. (20) "Lucky is being a parrot."

(21) Lucky just coughed.

---

1. What change should be made in sentence 1?
   Ⓐ Change <u>nilda</u> to <u>Nilda</u>.
   Ⓑ Change <u>had</u> to <u>have</u>.
   Ⓒ Change <u>pet</u> to <u>Pet</u>.
   Ⓓ Make no change.

2. What change should be made in sentence 2?
   Ⓐ Change <u>The</u> to <u>the</u>.
   Ⓑ Change <u>was</u> to <u>were</u>.
   Ⓒ Change <u>lucky</u> to <u>Lucky</u>.
   Ⓓ Make no change.

3. What change should be made in sentence 4?
   Ⓐ Change <u>Nilda</u> to <u>nilda</u>.
   Ⓑ Change <u>thought</u> to <u>thinked</u>.
   Ⓒ Change <u>Lucky</u> to <u>lucky</u>.
   Ⓓ Change <u>were</u> to <u>was</u>.

4. What change should be made in sentence 5?
   Ⓐ Change <u>she</u> to <u>it</u>.
   Ⓑ Change <u>taked</u> to <u>took</u>.
   Ⓒ Change <u>Dr.</u> to <u>dr</u>.
   Ⓓ Make no change.

5. What change should be made in sentence 6?
   Ⓐ Change <u>torres</u> to <u>Torres</u>.
   Ⓑ Change <u>doctor</u> to <u>Doctor</u>.
   Ⓒ Change <u>was</u> to <u>were</u>.
   Ⓓ Make no change.

6. What change should be made in sentence 7?
   Ⓐ Change <u>Dr.</u> to <u>dr</u>.
   Ⓑ Change <u>Torres</u> to <u>torres</u>.
   Ⓒ Change <u>looks</u> to <u>looked</u>.
   Ⓓ Change <u>Lucky</u> to <u>lucky</u>.

7. What change should be made in sentence 9?
   Ⓐ Change <u>How</u> to <u>how</u>.
   Ⓑ Change <u>feel</u> to <u>feeled</u>.
   Ⓒ Change the period to a question mark.
   Ⓓ Make no change.

8. What change should be made in sentence 10?
   Ⓐ Change <u>I</u> to <u>i</u>.
   Ⓑ Change <u>dont</u> to <u>don't</u>.
   Ⓒ Change <u>feel</u> to <u>felt</u>.
   Ⓓ Make no change.

9. What change should be made in sentence 17?
   Ⓐ Change <u>Nilda</u> to <u>nilda</u>.
   Ⓑ Change <u>to</u> to <u>two</u>.
   Ⓒ Change <u>to</u> to <u>too</u>.
   Ⓓ Make no change.

10. What change should be made in sentence 19?
    Ⓐ Change <u>isn't</u> to <u>isnt</u>.
    Ⓑ Change <u>isn't</u> to <u>i'snt</u>.
    Ⓒ Change <u>isn't</u> to <u>is'nt</u>.
    Ⓓ Make no change.

Read the story about a special kind of party.
Then answer questions 11–20.

Family Reunion

(1) My family had a reunion last summer. (2) Do you know what a reunion is. (3) A reunion is when everyone in a family gets together. (4) It is like a big party.

(5) People came from far away. (6) My grandmother came from Texas. (7) My aunt and uncle came from new york. (8) My great aunt came from Florida. (9) I did'nt know everyone. (10) I met many knew cousins.

(11) The reunion was in july. (12) It started on saturday. (13) We went to Silver Beach. (14) We swam in the see. (15) We played games. (16) I played soccer with my cousins. (17) I and my cousins played volleyball.

(18) A big cookout were planned. (19) I ate three hot dog. (20) We had ice cream and cake. (21) Everyone had fun.

(22) Then we said good-bye. (23) We will see each other again next year.

11. What change should be made in sentence 2?
   Ⓐ Change <u>Do</u> to <u>do</u>.
   Ⓑ Change <u>know</u> to <u>no</u>.
   Ⓒ Change <u>is</u> to <u>are</u>.
   Ⓓ Change the period to a question mark.

12. What change should be made in sentence 7?
   Ⓐ Change <u>aunt</u> to <u>Aunt</u>.
   Ⓑ Change <u>came</u> to <u>comed</u>.
   Ⓒ Change <u>new york</u> to <u>New York</u>.
   Ⓓ Change <u>new york</u> to <u>New york</u>.

13. What change should be made in sentence 9?
   Ⓐ Change did'nt to di'dnt.
   Ⓑ Change did'nt to didn't.
   Ⓒ Change I to i.
   Ⓓ Change know to no.

14. What change should be made in sentence 10?
   Ⓐ Change I to i.
   Ⓑ Change met to meeted.
   Ⓒ Change knew to new.
   Ⓓ Change cousins to cousin.

15. What change should be made in sentence 11?
   Ⓐ Change july to July.
   Ⓑ Change was to were.
   Ⓒ Change The to the.
   Ⓓ Make no change.

16. What change should be made in sentence 12?
   Ⓐ Change It to it.
   Ⓑ Change started to starts.
   Ⓒ Change saturday to Saturday.
   Ⓓ Make no change.

17. What change should be made in sentence 14?
   Ⓐ Change We to we.
   Ⓑ Change see to sea.
   Ⓒ Change swam to swimmed.
   Ⓓ Make no change.

18. What change should be made in sentence 17?
   Ⓐ Change I to i.
   Ⓑ Change played to play.
   Ⓒ Change I and my cousins to My cousins and I.
   Ⓓ Make no change.

19. What change should be made in sentence 18?
   Ⓐ Change planned to plans.
   Ⓑ Change were to was.
   Ⓒ Change big to Big.
   Ⓓ Make no change.

20. What change should be made in sentence 19?
   Ⓐ Change I to i.
   Ⓑ Change ate to eat.
   Ⓒ Change hot dog to Hot Dog.
   Ⓓ Change hot dog to hot dogs.

PART II

In Lessons 31–34 you write. Use what you've learned in Part I to *WRITE!*

DESCRIPTIONS

How can you tell someone how something looks? You can write a **description**. A good description helps readers see what you are writing about.

Here is a prompt for writing a description.

> *Describe a pair of shoes.*

Read the description. Read the Writing Tips. They will tell you about this kind of writing.

Writing Tips

* Use words that tell how something looks.

* Use words that tell how something sounds.

* Use words that tell how something feels.

* Use words that tell how something smells.

My shoes are basketball shoes. They are white and red. They have two straps that stick together. The straps go *rrrrip* when I pull them apart. The tops of my shoes feel smooth. The bottoms feel bumpy. My shoes smelled clean and leathery when they were new. Now they smell like stinky feet. My basketball shoes are special. No one else has a pair like them!

USING GRAPHIC ORGANIZERS

Graphic organizers help you get ready to write. The writer of the description on page 68 used a Word Web. Read the description again. Then complete the Word Web.

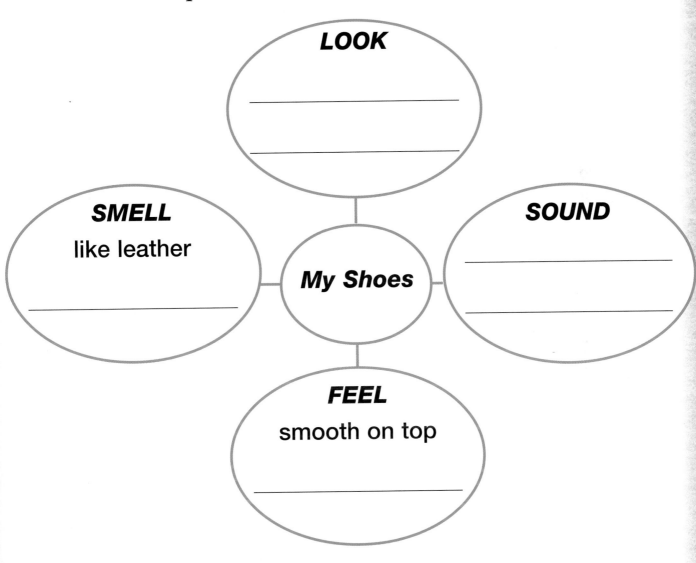

LOOK

_____

_____

SMELL

like leather

_____

My Shoes

SOUND

_____

_____

FEEL

smooth on top

_____

A Word Web helps writers think of the best words to describe something.

WRITING A DESCRIPTION

Now it is your turn to write a description. Use the prompt.

> *Describe a pair of shoes.*

THINK

Think about the shoes you want to write about. Use this graphic organizer to plan your writing. Write or draw how the shoes look, feel, smell, and sound.

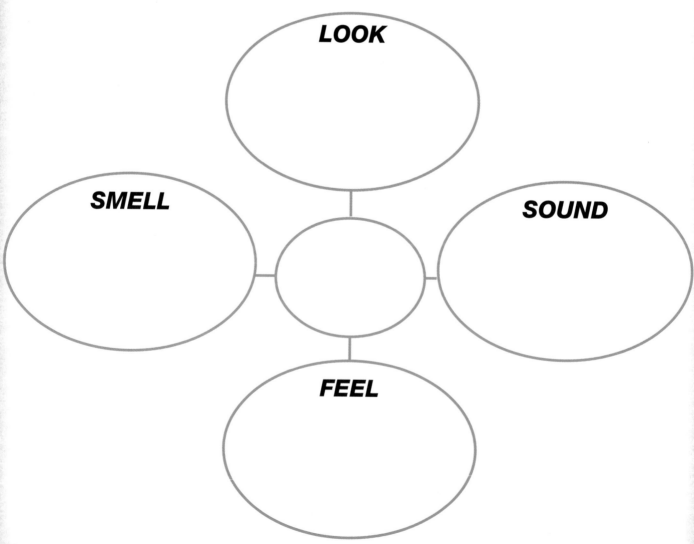

Use your graphic organizer to write your description. Write it on a sheet of paper.

Read what you wrote. Use this checklist to help you make your writing better.

I wrote about a pair of shoes. _____

I told how the shoes look, feel, smell, and sound. _____

My words will help readers see the shoes in their mind. _____

Make any changes that will make your description better.

LISTEN

Read your description to a partner.
Ask your partner these questions.
Carefully listen to the answers.

▲ Can you see what I described?

▲ Which sentence do you like best?

▲ What should I add to my description?

CHECK

Now it is time to check your writing.
Use this checklist to help you.
Answer each question.

Checking My Writing

Did I use plural nouns correctly? _____

Did I use special verbs correctly? _____

Does each sentence have a naming part
and an action part? _____

Did I begin each sentence with a capital letter? _____

WRITE AGAIN

Write a clean copy of your description.
Use another sheet of paper.

THINK ABOUT YOUR WRITING

**You have written a description! Think about
what you have learned. Finish these sentences.**

The best part of my description is _____

_____ .

The hardest part of writing a description was _____

_____ .

The sentence I like most is _____

_____ .

Next time I want to describe _____

_____ .

◆ ◆

Making Connections

◆ Draw a picture. Show what you described
in your writing. Does your picture show
everything that you described?

◆ Read your description to a partner.
Ask your partner to draw what you described.

INSTRUCTIONS

How do you play a game? How do you bake a cake? Instructions tell you how. Instructions tell you what to do first, next, and last.

Here is a prompt for writing instructions.

> *Write instructions that tell how to make a healthy snack.*

Read the instructions. Read the Writing Tips. They will tell you about this kind of writing.

Writing Tips

✳ Tell what to do in the right order.

✳ Use the words <u>first</u>, <u>next</u>, and <u>last</u>.

✳ Be sure to put all of the steps in. Don't forget any.

How to Make a Healthy Snack

The snack I make is an apple with peanut butter. First, I ask a grown-up to cut an apple. Next, I spread some peanut butter on each piece of apple. I use a spoon to spread the peanut butter. I cover each piece. Last, I put the apple pieces in a circle on a plate. I like this healthy snack. I think you will like it too.

USING GRAPHIC ORGANIZERS

Graphic organizers help you get ready to write. The writer of "How to Make a Healthy Snack" used a Step-by-Step Chart. Read "How to Make a Healthy Snack" again. Then complete the Step-by-Step Chart.

FIRST

Ask a grown-up to cut an apple.

_____

NEXT

Spread peanut butter on the apple.

_____

LAST

_____

_____

A Step-by-Step Chart helps writers plan the steps in instructions.

WRITING INSTRUCTIONS

Now it is your turn to write instructions.
Use the prompt.

> *Write instructions that tell how to make*
> *a healthy snack.*

THINK

Think about the snack you will write about.
Use this graphic organizer to plan
your writing. Write or draw each step.

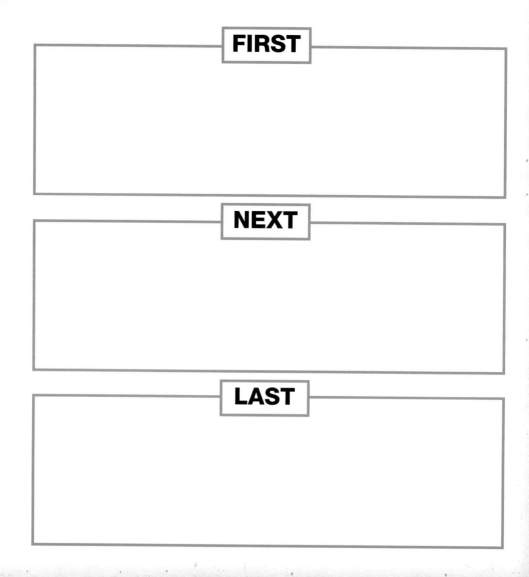

FIRST

NEXT

LAST

Use your graphic organizer to write your instructions. Write them on a sheet of paper.

Read what you wrote.
Use this checklist to help you make your writing better.

My instructions tell how to make a snack.   _____

The steps are in the correct order.   _____

I use the words <u>first</u>, <u>next</u>, and <u>last</u>.   _____

Make any changes that will make your instructions better.

LISTEN

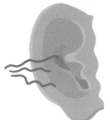

Read your instructions to a partner.
Ask your partner these questions.
Carefully listen to the answers.

▲ Are my steps in the right order?
▲ What do you like best about my instructions?
▲ What should I add to my instructions?

CHECK

Now it is time to check your writing.
Use this checklist to help you.

Checking My Writing

Did I use plural nouns correctly?　　　　　_____

Did I use <u>is</u> and <u>are</u> correctly?　　　　　_____

Did I use the correct homophone?　　　　　_____

Did I end each statement with a period?　　　　　_____

WRITE AGAIN

Now write a clean copy of your instructions.
Use another sheet of paper.

THINK ABOUT YOUR WRITING

**You have written instructions! Think about
what you have learned. Finish these sentences.**

The best part of my instructions is _____

_____ .

The hardest part of writing instructions was _____

_____ .

Next time I want to tell how to _____

_____ .

◆◆

Making Connections

◆ Read each step aloud. Have a classmate pretend
to make your snack.

◆ Draw a comic strip. Show three parts. Cut the pictures
apart and mix them up. Ask a partner to put the pictures
in the correct order.

BOOK REPORTS

What is your favorite book? What would you tell a friend about this book? You can write a book report to tell about a book you like.

Here is a prompt for writing a book report.

> *Write a book report about a book you have read.*

Read the book report. Read the Writing Tips. They will tell you more about writing a book report.

Writing Tips

❋ Tell the name of the book.

❋ Tell who wrote the book. This is the author.

❋ Tell what the book is about.

❋ Explain why you like the book.

I read <u>Splish, Splash!</u> The person who wrote the book is Sarah Weeks. The book is about animals in a tub. Lots of animals get into a tub. The animals are big and small. There is no room for a tiny bug. The animals squish to make room. Then the bug gets in the tub too. I like this book because the animals have a lot of fun.

USING GRAPHIC ORGANIZERS

Graphic organizers help you get ready to write.
The writer of the book report on page 80 used
a Book Report Chart. Read the book report again.
Then complete the Book Report Chart.

Title: <u>Splish, Splash!</u>

Author: Sarah Weeks

The book is about _____

_____

_____

_____ .

I like this book because _____

_____

_____

_____ .

*A Book Report Chart helps writers
remember what to put in a book report.*

WRITING A BOOK REPORT

Now it is your turn to write a book report.
Use the prompt.

> *Write a book report about a book you have read.*

 **THINK**

First, think of a book you like. Use this graphic organizer to plan your writing.

Title: _____

Author: _____

The book is about _____
_____
_____ .

I like this book because _____
_____
_____ .

Use your graphic organizer to write your book report. Write it on a sheet of paper.

Read what you wrote.
Use this checklist to help you make your writing better.

My book report tells the name of the book. _____

My book report tells who wrote the book. _____

I tell what happens in the book. _____

I tell why I like this book. _____

Make any changes that will make your book report better.

LISTEN

Read your book report to a partner.
Ask your partner these questions.
Carefully listen to the answers.

▲ What do you like best about my book report?

▲ What else would you like to know about this book?

CHECK

Now it is time to check your writing.
Use this checklist to help you.

Checking My Writing

Did I use capital letters correctly? _____

Did I use pronouns correctly? _____

Did I use an apostrophe to take the place of the <u>o</u> in contractions? _____

WRITE AGAIN

Now write a clean copy of your book report.
Use another sheet of paper.

THINK ABOUT YOUR WRITING

**You have written a book report! Think about
what you have learned. Finish these sentences.**

The best part of my book report is _____

_____ .

The hardest part of writing a book report was _____

_____ .

I should have told more about _____

_____ .

The next time I write a book report, I will remember to

_____ .

◆◆ Making Connections

◆ Did your book have pictures? Did you like the pictures?
Why or why not?

◆ Give a book talk. Tell a partner about your book.
Point to the book as you talk. Don't tell the ending!

◆ Read another book by the same author. How are
the two books alike? How are the two books different?

STORIES

You read and listen to stories every day at school. Writers wrote these stories. They wanted to share the stories with you. You can write stories too. Then other people can read your story!

Here is a prompt for writing a story.

> *Write a story about a child who loses a tooth.*

Read the story. Read the Writing Tips. They will teach you more about this kind of writing.

Writing Tips

✳ Think of a title for your story.

✳ Be sure your story has a beginning, a middle, and an ending.

✳ Tony is this story's most important character. Every story has a main character.

Tony's Loose Tooth

Tony's front tooth was loose. He wiggled it with his finger. He wiggled it again. His loose tooth would not come out. Tony ate a sandwich. His tooth was still there. Tony chewed popcorn. His tooth was still there. Tony brushed his teeth. His tooth was still there. He went to sleep. His tooth stayed in his mouth all night. Tony's mother knew what to do. She gave Tony a juicy, red apple. Tony bit into the apple, and then he smiled. His tooth was not loose any more. It was out!

USING GRAPHIC ORGANIZERS

Graphic organizers help you get ready to write. The writer of "Tony's Loose Tooth" used a Story Map. Read the story again. Write or draw what happens in the middle of the story.

BEGINNING

Tony's front tooth is loose.

MIDDLE

ENDING

Tony takes a bite of an apple.
His tooth comes out.

A Story Map helps writers plan a story.

Now it is your turn to write a story. Use the prompt.

Write a story about a child who loses a tooth.

THINK

First think about the story you want to tell. Then write or draw what happens in the beginning, middle, and ending of your story.

BEGINNING

MIDDLE

ENDING

Use your graphic organizer to write your story. Write it on a sheet of paper.

Now read your story. Use this checklist to help you make your story better.

My story has a title. _____

My story has a main character. _____

My story has a beginning. _____

My story has a middle. _____

My story has an ending. _____

Make any changes that will make your story better.

LISTEN

Read your story to a partner.
Ask your partner these questions.
Carefully listen to the answers.
▲ What do you like best about my story?
▲ Should I add anything to my story?
▲ Should I take anything out of my story?

CHECK

Now it is time to check your writing.
Use this checklist to help you.

Checking My Writing

Did I use verbs correctly?　　　　　　　　　　_____

Does each sentence have a naming part
and an action part?　　　　　　　　　　　　_____

Did I use a period or a question mark
at the end of each sentence?　　　　　　　　_____

Did I put capital letters where they belong?　_____

WRITE AGAIN

Now write a clean copy of your story.
Use another sheet of paper.

THINK ABOUT YOUR WRITING

**You have written a story! Think about what
you have learned. Finish these sentences.**

The best part of my story is _____

_____ .

One thing I changed to make my story better was _____

_____ .

One thing I added to my story to make it better was ____

_____ .

Next time, I want to write a story about _____

_____ .

◆◆

Making Connections

◆ Could your story be a play? What would your characters say? What would they wear? What scenery would you need?

◆ Write each sentence of your story on a sheet of paper. Draw a picture to go with each sentence. Write your title on a sheet of paper. Staple or fasten the pages together.

◆ Tell your story aloud to your classmates. How can your voice help make the story interesting?

On pages 92–95 are some writing prompts that you might see on tests. Read each prompt. The tips will help you write.

Prompt 1: Describe your favorite toy.

Tips

▲ Read the prompt carefully.

▲ Think about your favorite toy.

   ▲ What does it look like?

   ▲ Does it make noise?

   ▲ How does it feel when you touch it?

▲ Use a graphic organizer to plan your writing. A Word Web can help you plan a description.

▲ Tell what toy you are describing.

▲ Use words that tell how your toy looks, sounds, feels, and smells.

▲ Check your description for mistakes.

   ▲ Did you end each statement with a period?

   ▲ Did you use <u>is</u> and <u>are</u> correctly?

   ▲ Did you use capital letters correctly?

Prompt 2: Write instructions that tell how to sharpen a pencil.

Tips

▲ Read the prompt carefully.

▲ Think about what you do when you sharpen a pencil.

  ▲ What do you do first?

  ▲ What do you do next?

  ▲ What do you do last?

▲ Use a graphic organizer to plan your writing.
  A Step-by-Step Chart can help you plan instructions.

▲ Tell what you are explaining how to do.

▲ Tell what to do in the right order.

▲ Use the words <u>first</u>, <u>next</u>, and <u>last</u>.

▲ Don't forget any steps.

▲ Check your instructions for mistakes.

  ▲ Are all words spelled correctly?

  ▲ Does each sentence have a naming part
    and an action part?

  ▲ Did you begin all sentences with a capital letter?

Prompt 3: Write a book report about a favorite book.

Tips

▲ Read the prompt carefully.

▲ Think about the book you will write about.

  ▲ Do you know the title of the book?

  ▲ Do you know the name of the author?

  ▲ Why is this book your favorite?

▲ Use a graphic organizer to help you plan your writing. A Book Report Chart can help you plan a book report.

▲ Tell the name of the book.

▲ Tell who wrote the book.

▲ Tell what the book is about.

▲ Explain why the book is your favorite.

▲ Check your book report for mistakes.

  ▲ Did you capitalize the first word, the last word, and all the important words in the title of your book?

  ▲ Did you underline the title of the book?

  ▲ Did you capitalize the first and last names of people?

Prompt 4: Write a story about an animal that can talk.

Tips

▲ Read the prompt carefully.

▲ Think about who the main character of your story will be.

▲ Think about what you will say in your story.

   ▲ What will happen in the beginning?

   ▲ What will happen in the middle?

   ▲ How will your story end?

▲ Use a graphic organizer to help you plan your writing. A Story Map can help you plan your story.

▲ Tell readers details about your main character.

▲ Give your story a title that will make people want to read your story.

▲ Check your story for mistakes.

   ▲ Does your story make sense?

   ▲ Did you begin each sentence with a capital letter?

   ▲ Does each sentence end with a period or a question mark?